LIFE IN A
ROMAN
FORT

JANE SHUTER

Heinemann

Customer Service   888–454–2279

Visit our website at www.heinemannlibrary.com

Produced for Heinemann Library by
    Bender Richardson White.
Photo research by Cathy Stastny and
    Maria Joannou
Designed by Ben White and
    Ron Kamen
Printed in China

09 08 07 06 05
10 9 8 7 6 5 4 3 2 1

**Library of Congress Cataloging-in-Publication
Data**

Shuter, Jane.
    Life in a Roman fort / Jane Shuter.
        p. cm. -- (Picture the past)
    Includes bibliographical references and index.
    ISBN 1-4034-5829-4 (hardcover) -- ISBN 1-4034-
5837-5 (pbk.)
    1. Fortification--Rome--Juvenile literature. 2.
Rome--Army--Juvenile literature. 3. Rome--Military
antiquities--Juvenile literature. 4. Excavations
(Archaeology)--Rome--Juvenile literature. I. Title.
II. Series.
    UG428.S53 2004
    355.7'0937--dc22
                                            2004002366

Acknowledgements:
The publishers would like to thank the following for
permission to reproduce photographs: Ancient
Art and Architecture/R. Sheridan pp. **6**, **8**, **10**, **14**,
15, **16**, **21**; Corbis Images Inc./Archivo
Iconografico, S. A. p. **7**; Corbis Images Inc./Jason
Hawkes p. **30**; David Cuzick /Visual Image p. **11**;
Duncan Gilbert p. **18**; Terry Griffiths/Magnet
Harlequin pp. **9**, **19**, **20**, **24**, **25**, **26**; Vindolanda
Trust pp. **22**, **23**, **28**; Werner Forman Archive p. **12**.

Cover photograph of Trajan's column
reproduced with permission of Ancient Art and
Architecture/R. Sheridan.

Some words are shown in bold, **like this**.
You can find out what they mean by
looking in the Glossary.

ABOUT THIS BOOK
This book is about daily life in **forts**
in Roman times. The Romans ruled
from about 753 B.C.E to 476 C.E. At
first, they ruled only the city of Rome,
in Italy, and the land around it.
However, they built a huge **empire**
by taking over more and more land
and ruling it with Roman **laws**. By
about 117 C.E. the Roman Empire
was huge. The Romans could not
have captured lands without their
army. They needed many soldiers
and forts to maintain the empire.
Many local people were unhappy
with Roman rule, and the army had
to keep them under control.

We have illustrated this book with
photographs of objects and forts from
Roman times. We have also used
artists' ideas of fort life. These
drawings are based on Roman forts
that have been found and
investigated by **archaeologists**.

The author
Jane Shuter is a professional writer and
editor of non-fiction books for children.
She graduated from Lancaster University in
1976 with a BA honours degree and then
earned a teaching qualification. She taught
from 1976 to 1983, changing to editing and
writing when her son was born. She lives in
Oxford with her husband and son.

Contents

Roman Forts

The Roman army built an **empire** of captured lands for Rome from 753 B.C.E. The Romans were not always welcome in the lands they took over. The army had to keep local people from taking back their lands. Its soldiers built a network of roads and **forts** to keep control of the empire. The army moved around to wherever trouble broke out. This was most likely in the places farthest from Rome, at the edges of the empire. In these places, Roman soldiers set up forts to protect its lands all year long.

Look for these: The fort shows you the subject of each double-page chapter in the book. The soldier's helmet shows you boxes with interesting facts, figures, and quotes about Roman forts.

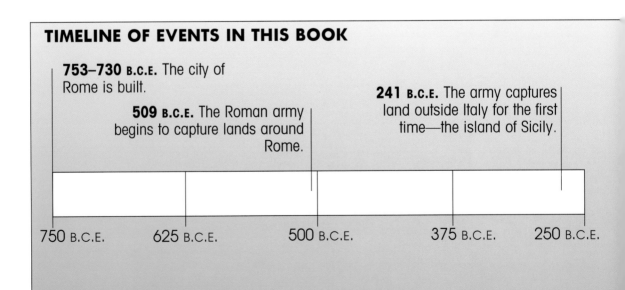

TIMELINE OF EVENTS IN THIS BOOK

753–730 B.C.E. The city of Rome is built.

509 B.C.E. The Roman army begins to capture lands around Rome.

241 B.C.E. The army captures land outside Italy for the first time—the island of Sicily.

750 B.C.E.   625 B.C.E.   500 B.C.E.   375 B.C.E.   250 B.C.E.

This map shows the Roman Empire at its biggest, in about 117 C.E. The lines show the main roads. There were many more roads than this. The dots show the biggest forts on the edges of the empire.

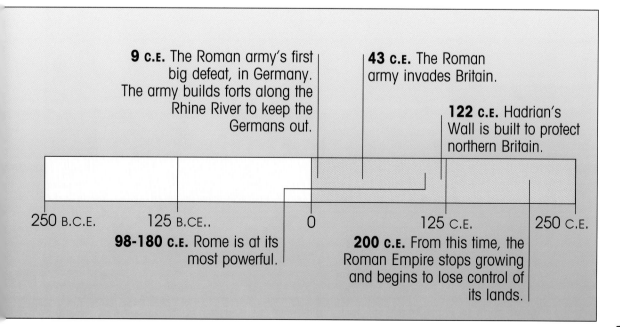

9 c.e. The Roman army's first big defeat, in Germany. The army builds forts along the Rhine River to keep the Germans out.

43 c.e. The Roman army invades Britain.

122 c.e. Hadrian's Wall is built to protect northern Britain.

250 B.C.E.　　125 B.CE..　　0　　125 C.E.　　250 C.E.

98-180 c.e. Rome is at its most powerful.

200 c.e. From this time, the Roman Empire stops growing and begins to lose control of its lands.

The Roman Army

The Roman army was very well organized. People who joined the army were put into groups of a hundred (a century) led by a **centurion.** Of the 100 men in a century, 80 were soldiers. The other 20 people kept the **records,** or had other skills the army needed—some were doctors, for example. Six centuries made up a **cohort.** Ten cohorts made a **legion.**

Soldiers trained to fight as a group. They practiced making this *testudo* (turtle-shaped) defense with their shields (below left), time and time again. Then, when they had to do it in battle, they could do it very quickly.

Roman soldiers had to be able to do everything for themselves. They were not just fighters. They had to be able to make a safe camp quickly every night and feed themselves there. They had to build more permanent **forts** in lands they took over—and roads to link these new lands to the **empire.**

THE ARMY

As the Roman Empire grew, it needed a full-time army. This was made up of:

- male Roman citizens who chose to join the army
- people from countries taken over by Rome who volunteered
- people captured during wars who were forced to join.

Roman soldiers moved around the empire by sea as well as by road. This carving shows soldiers on a ship.

The Edge of Empire

As the Roman **Empire** grew, soldiers had to live farther and farther away from Rome. The Romans went as far north as Great Britain. They started building Hadrian's Wall, for the Roman **emperor** Hadrian, in 122 C.E. They finished it in about 135 C.E. The wall marked the northern edge of the empire. It had **forts** along it and could be crossed only at guarded crossing places known as milecastles.

Hadrian's Wall was not built all at once, from one side to the other. It was built in sections. When it was finished, it stretched 73 miles (117 kilometers), from one side of Great Britain to the other. There were sixteen forts, in all, along Hadrians' Wall.

Soldiers came to the forts on Hadrian's Wall from all over the empire. Many came from northern Europe—from what is now Germany and Belgium. The Roman army did have British soldiers, but they were sent to other countries, not kept in Britain. The **praetor,** commander in charge of the fort, was usually a Roman citizen, because the Romans did not completely trust local people.

LETTERS HOME

Over 300 Roman documents were found at Vindolanda Fort on Hadrian's Wall. Some list **stores.** Others are letters. One letter to an ordinary soldier says, "I have sent you some socks, two pairs of sandals, and two pairs of underpants."

On Hadrian's Wall in Great Britain, each **legion** built about 5 miles (8 kilometers) of wall. They carved certain stones along the wall to say which legion, or part of a legion, built that section.

Building the Fort

When Roman soldiers first captured an area of land, they built a temporary **fort** from the poles they carried. Then they built permanent forts, with walls and deep ditches on either side for safety. Forts were often built as part of a long defensive wall. If so, the wall also had smaller forts, called milecastles, dotted along them.

This famous Roman carving, called Trajan's Column, shows soldiers doing building work as well as fighting. Each **legion** had an **engineer.** He made sure that the forts were built properly.

The soldiers sometimes used local people to dig up and carry the stone for forts and walls, but they did most of the building work themselves. Forts were the same all over the **empire.** The headquarters, the place where the weapons and money were kept, were always in the middle of the fort, facing the main entrance.

In this fort, near the front there are barracks for soldiers. The headquarters are in the center, with a hospital and storehouse on the left, and the praetor's quarters and other officers on the right. At the back there are workshops and stables for the horses.

IN A FORT

Forts were often on a long defensive wall. They each had:
- a headquarters
- a house for the **praetor** in charge and his family
- **barracks** for the soldiers. Most forts held 800 to 1,000 soldiers.
- a toilet block
- a bath house, usually outside the walls of the fort
- workshops around the walls
- milecastles between the forts.

Roads

Roads were very important to the army. Soldiers and supplies could move around more easily on dry, paved roads. Roads were built higher in the middle and sloped on either side. The low sides, or drains, took away the water that ran off the road. Using these roads, messengers could take orders from Rome to all parts of the **empire.** They could cover about 150 miles (240 kilometers) a day.

Ordinary people also used Roman roads. Traders carried all kinds of goods from one part of the empire to another. Places to eat and sleep were built along the busiest roads.

Soldiers built the roads, using local workers for digging and carrying. First, workers dug a trench about 6 feet (1.8 meters) deep. They flattened the earth at the bottom, adding a layer of sand. Then they placed big stones on top of this, holding them together with **cement.** Next they placed a layer of smaller stones and cement, then gravel, then sand and cement. Last, they put on a top layer of big, flat stones.

ROAD WORKS

Roman roads were very well made. The engineers changed how deep the layers were depending on how wet the soil was. Some Roman roads still exist today, although most have been built over.

Engineers marked a route for the road. Workers pounded down each layer with a heavy stone on a pole while the cement was still wet. This made the road last a long time.

Work

Roman soldiers were sent to **forts** like those on Hadrian's Wall for years at a time. They spent very little time fighting, but they did drill exercises, practicing fighting moves, every day. Because Roman soldiers fought as a group, they had to be able to move their spears, swords, and shields at exactly the same time, to stop them from hurting each other by accident. The soldiers also spent time keeping their weapons and armor in good condition.

The army thought it was important for soldiers to lood good. They had to polish their helmets until they shined. They had special helmets, like this one, to wear for important events such as a visit by the **emperor.**

As well as building roads, forts, and walls, soldiers had long lists of duties. Aside from training, which they did all the time, they had different duties each week. They checked everyone who wanted to go from one side of the wall to the other. They went out on **patrols,** exploring the enemy side of the wall. Some of the soldiers helped the local workers who made and fixed the armor and equipment.

The army mostly bought its food from the local people. If people refused to sell them food, the soldiers took what they needed. Each soldier carried a sickle to cut **grain**—as shown in this carving—that was ground into flour for bread.

Clothes and Armor

Soldiers wore **linen** underwear with a red **tunic** on top. In colder places, they also wore pants to just below the knee. Their boots had nails on the bottom to get a good grip in the mud or on slippery grass. Soldiers wore a helmet and armor to protect their shoulders and upper body—the parts most likely to get hit in battle.

INJURY POINTS

Armor was made out of strips of metal in layers, so the soldiers could move more easily. However, lower arms and legs were left bare and often got injured.

Swords, like these gladii, needed to be kept sharp. Water troughs all over the **empire** had grooves in the stone around them. Soldiers sharpened their swords and daggers there by moving them back and forth in the stone grooves.

16

Pilum, or spear

Body armor

Helmet

Pickaxe

Basket

Pole

Gladius, or sword

Shield

A Roman soldier's equipment weighed about 77 pounds (35 kilograms). He had to carry or wear it while marching. He had:

- a long spear, called a pilum, for stabbing and throwing
- a sword, called a gladius, for stabbing
- a shield with a different pattern on for each **cohort**
- body armor and a helmet
- up to four long poles, to make a camp for the night
- a basket to carry a cooking pot
- a tin plate
- a small grindstone (to grind corn into flour), a sickle to cut corn, a saw, and a pickaxe.

Health and Hygiene

The Romans wanted a healthy army. Sick soldiers cannot fight. Because soldiers lived crowded together in **barracks,** illnesses spread very quickly. The Romans knew that dirty conditions could help spread disease. So soldiers were expected to keep very clean. They had to wash themselves and their clothes regularly. Every **fort** had toilets and bath houses.

These Roman toilets show the stone seats and a drain at ground level. The drain had clean water running in it, so people could rinse the sponges they used as toilet paper.

TOILETS

The toilets were in a large room with wooden seats around the sides. In the middle was a big tub of water for hand washing. Sponges on sticks were used as toilet paper, and then washed and reused. Then the dirty water washed down the drain.

Each century had a doctor in charge of medical care. The doctor had several helpers. They worked as nurses, cleaning and bandaging wounds and giving patients medicines. Doctors also treated day-to-day problems, such as boils (swollen areas on the skin), sore teeth, burns, and eye infections. They used herbs to make medicines and ointments.

These surgeon's tools were found at Corbridge Fort on Hadrian's Wall. They were used for small operations, such as clearing out boils.

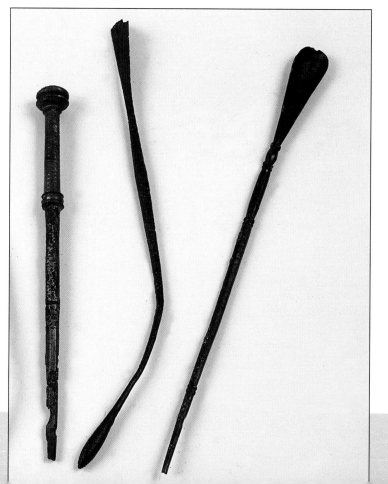

Barracks

When soldiers were on the move, they slept in tents, with eight in each tent. In **forts** they lived in **barracks,** which had room for up to 100 soldiers. Barracks were long buildings divided up to give each tent its own area of about 22 feet (6.8 meters) by 12 feet (3.6 meters). This area had two rooms, one for sleeping in and one for the soldiers' equipment.

These barracks at Housesteads Fort on Hadrian's Wall were built as long buildings, one to each **cohort**. In about 300 C.E., they were rebuilt as eight separate blocks, with small lanes between them.

Barracks had only the most basic furniture. The army did not want soldiers to be too comfortable, or to spend too long in barracks. However, the army wanted healthy soldiers, so barracks were well built and did not leak or have drafts. Many barracks had fireplaces, to keep the soldiers warm and dry. A covered porch ran along one side, to give some covered outside space.

NO PRIVACY

The **centurion** had his own room at one end of the barracks. But ordinary soldiers had no privacy at all. They lived together and ate together. The army wanted them to think of themselves as part of a team all the time.

Barracks had only small windows, so they were often dark. Lamps like these, filled with oil, were burned for light, but they only gave a dim light, and often gave off a lot of smoke.

Family Life

Only the **praetor** in charge of the **fort**, who had his own house, was allowed to have his family living with him. The praetor's wife led a lonely life, with only her **slaves** for female company in the fort. **Officers'** families sometimes followed them and lived in nearby towns. These officers had to get permission to visit their families in their time off.

WIVES' LIVES

Sulpicia, the wife of the praetor of Vindolanda Fort, made friends with Claudia, the wife of an army officer. They wrote and visited each other. Claudia invited Sulpicia to her birthday party, "Make sure you come. I will enjoy it more if you are there."

Sulpicia and her husband Ceralis had children while they were living at Vindolanda Fort. This child's shoe was found in their house.

Regular soldiers had to leave their families behind when they joined the army. They were expected to live and work as a group, with the army as their family. Sometimes soldiers married local women, or their families moved to be near them. Even so, the soldiers could only visit them with special permission from the praetor.

Carved pieces of the gemstone jet, like this one, were often given when two people agreed to marry. Despite army disapproval, soldiers did marry and have families.

Off-Duty Activities

Soldiers did get some time off. They had to get permission to leave the **fort,** and had to be back by a set time. If a fort was a long way from a town, a small town was built around it. Local people set up shops selling food and drink, pottery, and cooking pots. There were workshops that made and repaired shoes and clothes.

In the ruins of the village outside Housesteads Fort, you can still see the groove that the big shutter at the front of this shop slid down into when the shop was shut up for the night.

The **praetor** and his **officers** visited each other and hired entertainers, such as dancers and acrobats, for parties. Regular soldiers who had families usually visited them when they had time off. Others went to inns or to the army bath house. In both these places they could gossip, eat, drink, and play games.

OLD SOLDIERS

Soldiers joined for 15 years, then could rejoin for 10 years at a time. After 25 years, retiring soldiers were given money for a farm or business. Some soldiers who had spent a long time in one place retired there and became part of the local community.

This board game and dice were found at Vindolanda Fort. The dice have been loaded—weights were put inside to make the numbers 1 and 6 come up most often.

25

Religion

The Romans worshipped many different gods and goddesses, who they believed controlled everyday life. So it was important to pray to the gods to keep them happy. Each **fort** had a room in the main building that held a **shrine** to the gods. There also were shrines and **temples** to the gods in the town outside the fort. Local gods were often worshipped here, too.

This altar to Mars, the god of war, was set up in Housesteads Fort. Mars was an important god for soldiers, who wanted him on their side in battle.

Many soldiers worshipped the god Mithras as a god of victory. Mithras was a sun god. He was worshipped secretly, unlike most Roman gods and goddesses. This means we do not know a lot about how soldiers worshipped Mithras, although we know he was important. We do not even know why they believed Mithras was different.

MITHRAS

There was a *mithraeum,* a temple to Mithras, at Housesteads Fort on Hadrian's Wall. An altar to Mithras was found there, put up by a soldier called Litorius Pacatianus. People often promised the gods to put up an altar if the gods helped them.

Most Romans worshipped outside temples and shrines, because only the priests could go inside. Because Mithras was worshipped in secret, everyone went into the temple, as this artist's view of a temple to Mithras shows.

Food

The Romans knew that eating right helped people stay healthy. So soldiers ate healthy food. They ate three meals a day together. They had bread, **porridge,** cheese, and plenty of fresh fruits and vegetables. They ate meat only occasionally. The meat came from animals they hunted, such as rabbits or wild pigs. Unless there was clean, fresh water available, they mostly drank wine.

In forts like Vindolanda, **grain** was ground for flour on large stone mills called querns. This is the bottom stone. Another stone was fixed on top of it and turned with a handle to grind the grain.

Roman recipe—army porridge

Roman soldiers used different sorts of **grains** to make their porridge. You can make a mix like their porridge using oat bran or, if you cannot find this, ground or rolled oats. Do not use instant oatmeal mix.

This recipe feeds about four people.

WARNING: Ask an adult to help you with the cooking.

1 Rub the bottom of the saucepan with a few drops of oil. Be sure to get into the edges.

2 Stir the oat bran or rolled oats and water together in a saucepan. Stir until it makes a thick paste.

3 Heat the saucepan gently—do not boil. At first, you do not have to stir all the time.

4 As the water gets hot, the oats will slowly swell up to make the mixture thicker.

5 Keep stirring until the mixture is as thick as a thick milkshake or a smoothie. It will take from 10 to 25 minutes of stirring.

When the Romans left a country they had taken over, their **forts** and walls were often reused by the local people. They moved into the forts to defend themselves against other groups of people. When the Roman buildings were no longer needed for defense, the stone from them was used for new buildings. Today, remains of Roman forts are still being uncovered when places are dug up to build new offices, shops, or homes.

REUSE OF STONES

To make their forts and walls, the Roman dug stones out of the ground and shaped them. So reusing the stones saved local builders much work.

Not all the stones from forts and walls were taken away. In some places, enough was left to figure out what the buildings had been. Now places like Housesteads Fort in Great Britain are visited each year by thousands of people.

Glossary

archaeologist person who uncovers old buildings and burial sites to find out about the past

barracks building in a fort in which soldiers live

cement mixture of lime, water, and powdered stone used for building, which dries into a hard material

centurion officer in charge of a century—about 80 soldiers and 20 workers—in the Roman army

cohort group of about 480 soldiers and 120 workers

emperor ruler of ancient Rome

empire country and all the other lands it controls

engineer person who knows how to build roads, buildings, and

bridges so they are safe and can take heavy loads

fort place built to keep people, usually soldiers, safe from attack

grain seeds of some grasses that can be eaten. Barley, wheat, rice, oats, and rye are all grains.

law rule made by the people running a country

legion group of about 4,800 soldiers and 1,200 workers

linen cloth made from flax

officer person in the army who is in charge of soldiers

patrol group of soldiers moving around the local area, making sure nothing goes on that could hurt the lives of Romans or the fort

porridge soft food made by cooking grains in liquid

praetor person in charge of a fort

record written list that shows how something is run

shrine place where people come to pray to gods and goddesses and leave them gifts

slave person who is bought and sold like property

stores things an army needs to keep it going, such as tools, food, and medicine

temple place where people pray to gods and goddesses

tunic T shirt-shaped clothing that comes down to about the knees, worn by Roman men, women and children

More Books to Read

James, Simon. *See Through History: Ancient Rome*. Chicago: Heinemann Library, 1996.

Reid, Struan. *The Life and World of Julius Caesar*. Chicago: Heinemann Library, 2002.

Williams, Brenda. *History of Britain: Roman Conquest of Britain*. Chicago: Heinemann Library, 1996.

Williams, Brian. *See Through History: Forts and Castles*. Chicago: Heinemann Library, 1994.

Index